THE DANCE

THE DANCE Copyright © 2023 by Art of Telling Publications, LLC. All rights reserved. No part of this publication may be used or reproduced in any manner whatsoever without written permission except in the case of brief quotations embodied in critical articles and reviews. For information address Art of Telling Publications, 2153 Rte. 35 N Holmdel, NJ 07733

Library of Congress Control Number: 2023917056

ISBN 978-17348447-4-0

10 9 8 7 6 5 4 3 2 1

Dedicated to the smile that no one else understands.

Also by Sea Gudinski:

1969: A BRIEF AND BEAUTIFUL TRIP BACK

A COLLECTION OF WORDS

SKULLS & ROSES

THE DANCE

SEA GUDINSKI

CONTENTS

VALENTINE'S DAY	13
FRONT SEAT CABARET	15
MEMORIES FOR SALE	18
I LOVE YOU TOO	19
AN UNTITLED WISH	20
I CAN'T HELP BUT BE SCARED OF IT ALL SOMETIMES	21
SEDUCTION	23
EMPTY BARSTOOL	25
DREAMING OF ELYSIUM FROM BEHIND A PLEXI-GLAS SCREEN	26
WHO ARE YOU LOVING, REALLY?	28
TO STROLL	30
GIN	33
O DEATH	35
LOVE AND OTHER HEARTACHES	39
3AM	42
THE ENIGMA	43
THE DANCE	47

THE DANCE

SEA GUDINSKI

THE DANCE

VALENTINE'S DAY

I asked the bartender to pour me another shot;
Gin pairs well with my soliloquy of pain.
The gin slides down easy,
The pain is a harder pill—
But I choke it down
With a glib remark
And a forced smile
As I sit
At an unfamiliar bar at eleven in the morning
Waiting
For the call that is keen to blow my life apart.

Once in a while,
Nowhere feels like home anymore.
If I could crawl out of my skin,
Leave my ravaged mind behind,
I'd crawl into your arms.
I'd follow you into the next life
And pray
That sins can be forgiven and that
Love can last.

Fear
Of the inevitable
Has aged me far beyond my years,
And as time
Has gone on and pleasures
Have set, the inevitable

VALENTINE'S DAY

Has always seemed
Equidistant.

The inevitable always
Comes knocking when it is least invited
And least expected.

THE DANCE

FRONT SEAT CABARET

Silhouettes—
dancing in silence—
or near silence—
in darkness interrupted by a streetlight—
unwillingly interrupted—
as it is the figures' prerogative to hide from eyes not their own.

But their eyes are hardly watching.

They're both looking for something—
comfort and promise, is it?
Safety?
To melt into one another and just be?
Just laugh and just love?

—And in one another, that is what they find.

What wonder,
what questions,
what words communicated only by a touch
and subsequently consumed.
Consumed by passion,
by need,
by desire.
To recount, neither dare.
To remember, both relish.

FRONT SEAT CABARET

But oh!
What fear exists—
what fear persists and proliferates.
What fear spurns
and is choked into silence with a scream.
What need is expressed in the same.

Oh! But how they dance despite the danger—
deftly skirting dashboard and console,
reclining seats to aid pleasure and accessibility,
dodging shifter and security camera.
Bending and stretching,
rising and gliding they weave their bodies together,
dipping and plunging—
holding one another so forbiddingly tight,
with hands entangled in hair and lips barely parted,
throwing lustful shadows into the ever-receptive night.

Together,
they cry out in voices laden with want and desire.
They are voices stifled by hopelessness and impossibility,
voices stricken with lies,
stricken with desperate vain hope that no one is looking,
hope that no one knows,
that no one thinks,
that no one unsuspectingly glances over

THE DANCE

FRONT SEAT CABARET

and points,
laughs,
and tells.
But they are voices satisfied,
oh so satisfied.

And
if any luckless passerby happened to hear
and glance nigh,
what they'd observe is no less than a front seat cabaret—
for fools only,
encores expected,
the price of admission: your soul.

SEA GUDINSKI

MEMORIES FOR SALE

Please do not touch
The hubcap in the basket
Or the crab trap on the shelf.

THE DANCE

I LOVE YOU TOO

To the one who looks through me—I've found asylum in your eyes.
Not asylum
Of the mind,
But asylum of the heart.
In you I
Have discovered a state of
Pure Love —
A Love nondependent
Upon position
Or praise,
Lifestyles
Or labels.
I have found Love that exists in the face of all sense and reason
And burns brightly
In the darkness of fear and uncertainty.
I have discovered a refuge for sin
And sacrifice.
In spite of all both
Wicked and righteous, we
Have one another.

AN UNTITLED WISH

I remember for some.
I forget for some.

For some, I spare words.
For others, expression flows. For me, I am. And for me, I write.

The intersection of souls serves as a catalyst of love—
Of passion—
Of faith—
That maybe, possibly, we are here for a reason other than to live and to die.

Rather, to record.
To learn something and leave behind something that can be learned from.

That we aren't just here to breathe for a while and then return to the sky...but to do something meaningful in between.

That maybe my life is more than just a glimmer in the sun, but maybe a glimmer in the night...

To show the way that I've been so some other soul may be spared the hazards of the road ahead of the journey,

And, in turn, he may journey further ahead on his own.

THE DANCE

I CAN'T HELP BUT BE SCARED OF IT ALL SOMETIMES

I love you.
I've never loved anyone more.
Thoughts of you fill my days, and your influence seeps into every crack of my life like rain.
You invigorate me, and you sustain me.
I need your presence like I need air to breathe.
I've never wanted to need.
I don't need anything—
except you.

I need you.
And nothing scares me more than the idea of losing you.
The thought of living without you feels to me like drowning...
but being with you feels like drowning too.
I am powerless in your presence.
With your kiss, you consume me;
and there is nothing more I want in those moments than to just melt away.
But I am not alone.

Nobody ever wants to let go.
Nobody ever wants to be the first to break an embrace with the one they love.
Nobody ever wants to think it may be the last time.
But sooner or later, it always will be.

SEA GUDINSKI

I CAN'T HELP BUT BE SCARED OF IT ALL SOMETIMES

So, remember,
but remember with a smile—
even if accompanied by tears.
For your past is the bones you're made of;
experience is the blood that runs through your veins;
and memories are the scarred skin that holds it all together.
To fear loss is to love, but it is also to forfeit living.
There are no 'see you laters', only goodbyes.
There are no guaranteed tomorrows, only right now.
So, either live or let it ride—because none of us get out alive.

THE DANCE

SEDUCTION

Part your lips and let me in,
you know I'm right outside.
I'll tell you that you can have
as much or as little of me as you please.
In the riddle of your life,
I will be your solution.
In the middle of the night,
when I call you awake from bed,
you will answer.
When I whisper your name at sunrise,
you'll caress me gently
and begin your day with the taste of me on your tongue.
You'll love me with your heart,
you'll love me with your soul.
You'll tell me you can't live without me,
you'll tell me you need me near.
You'll call me your angel,
your savior,
and there in the glass I will shine.
You will find me the anodyne of your every ill;
the subtle embrace that quells your every fear.
When you cry,
I'll be there.
When you rejoice,
I'll be there.

SEDUCTION

When you feel you have nothing left,
when you have sacrificed your soul to my intoxicating will,
I will be your comfort,
your redeemer.

And I will lie.
I will lie with words so sweet and convincing that they will
pierce you
and bleed you
and you'll scream with the pleasure of my touch.
I am a secret most indelible,
an indulgence so poignant—
and by the time you realize you need me,
it'll be far too late to leave me.

THE DANCE

EMPTY BARSTOOL

Stepping through the threshold of days gone by,
your laugh echoes from the walls,
your smile reflects from every mirror.
Your touch caresses me like a ghost every time someone opens the back door
and the warm wind swirls around me.
There's not a man alive who can recreate a moment,
but boy how a song can resurrect a memory—
and with what force.
Just makes me want to breathe—
inhale every last lingering vestige of what once was.
Makes me want to melt
and makes me want to swear.
Makes me want to cry in remorse
and makes me want to dance—
slow and sweet and full of purpose and emotion.
It makes me want to dance with vigor
and clutch that which I love close to me with every ounce of my strength,
but I come up with empty arms.
There's a fullness in my heart for you,
but you're not here.
I look through the lens of love,
but you are nowhere to be seen.
And how incredibly empty that feels—like I'm peering through a vacant picture frame and into real life.

SEA GUDINSKI

DREAMING OF ELYSIUM FROM BEHIND A PLEXI-GLAS SCREEN

And we'll shatter the glass and
the reflection of the lights and
all things like them that distort the purity of life,
that diminish it,
cheapen it,
and make it seem less than what it is.
We'll do away with the hideous masks that people
pull down over their faces
to conceal their true expressions—
their crooked smiles,
their laughter,
their hidden contempt.
We'll eliminate
the space that we maintain between one another,
and all men's souls will sigh
and remember that we're all one.
No one gets out alive;
instead of dying every day,
we need to live with joy and
grace and
gratitude.
Instead of crawling on our bellies
though the excrement of the world,
we should run—
run into the arms of one another.
Instead of asking why,
we should dance.

THE DANCE

DREAMING OF ELYSIUM FROM BEHIND A PLEXI-GLAS SCREEN

Instead of fighting,
we should love.
Instead of mourning loss,
we should live life.

WHO ARE YOU LOVING, REALLY?

Who do you think of
when you make love to me?

Do you think of all the loves you've loved before
—those loves you can never love again?

Do you consider in the midst of a kiss
—a touch—
love that's wilted
and faded
but not yet died away?
Love you wish to rekindle?
Love that's locked up tight in the cask of time
inside some soft beating heart that isn't mine?

Do you remember the loves of youth?
Does my love instill memories in your breast? Memories you
wish to relive?

Is that name you hesitate to call mine after all?

When you close your eyes,
is it my face that you see?

When you reach out to embrace me,
is it my hand that you grasp?

THE DANCE

WHO ARE YOU LOVING, REALLY?

To whom do your affections belong?
Are they stirred by the one to whom they are given,
or am I a passion surrogate?

Anticipation may well be the greatest aphrodisiac
—but for whom are you waiting?

How does such a seasoned lover cross the gulf of fear and guilt
so willingly if you are not,
in some manner,
attempting to unite its shores?

And in these fleeting wisps of time
wherein we get to wrap one another in our longing arms,
why can't I believe it is me that you desire to hold?

You say you wish we could run away,
but who are you running to?

You say you wish you could make me yours,
but what would that make you?

I'd love to make love to you,
but who are you loving, really?

SEA GUDINSKI

TO STROLL

A form-fitting figure
stands at the precipice of truth and doubt;
of lies and revelation.
As my eyes rest upon him,
I ask myself:
Shall I cast myself out across the sky in a spectacle for all to see?
—A burning, trembling star to fall?
Or do I remain cloistered on the dock of desire?
—Hemmed in by moral clarity, social pressures, and shame?
Should I turn and walk away in search of greener pastures
untainted by lechery?

Resonance is abundant in the human heart
and freely abounds when given license.
But what license is given
to those who hinder themselves?
What license is given
to those who are trapped,
netted,
and confined by their own emotions—
unable to be expressed
out of fear of the backlash
from a culture unwilling to admit

THE DANCE

TO STROLL

that such desires exist within all of us
and at one time or another
long to be expressed.
Temptation does not solely afflict the weak,
but it is the proud who refuse to recognize its influence.

When words flow like water
and laughter alights the wind,
when gazes linger longer
and the touch of gentle embraces smolder
like an ember desperate to reignite,
logic no longer reigns.
Turning and walking away becomes near impossible—
especially in such desirable proximity.

To assert that I have grasped
at the very dregs of resolve in an attempt to arrest desire
would be a gross exaggeration.

So,
for now,
sensory titillation, do your magic.
Traipse across my skin
like a ballerina on thin ice.
Mount my mind
like a jockey on a winning stud.
Take my hand
and let us dance through the minefield.

SEA GUDINSKI

TO STROLL

Together,
let us find the terminus of a dream
and let us awake once we are abreast of its ending.

A stroll through the woods
on a cool, clear summer morning.
It doesn't seem possible
that such treason can be committed in such beautiful
and unsuspecting surroundings.

Oh desire,
what nefarious crimes
are committed in your name.

THE DANCE

GIN

In the early morning,
when whereupon rising,
I see the sun,
I thank the Lord
and take a shot.
In the early morning,
when whereupon rising,
rain falls down,
I curse the devil
and take a shot.

At the close of the day,
tired and content,
I sigh with a smile
and fill my glass to the brim.
At the close of the day,
tired and weary,
I sigh with a grimace
and I fill my glass to the brim.

In moments of levity and celebration,
I crack open a bottle
and toast to good health and fortune.
In moments of grief and despair,
I crack open a bottle
and drink to forget the fear.

SEA GUDINSKI

GIN

Gin—

It erodes reason
like a sand sculpture
in a rushing tide.
Blithely curious,
it sensually winds its way around the tongue
until the unsuspecting organ can do no more
than thoughtlessly carry out its new master's wanton bidding.
It is as sinful as Satan's snake
and yet as poised and proper
as the queen depicted on its cask.
Innocence dies with the first swallow,
the second lends itself to awful foreboding,
and the third nearly whisks you away to paradise
where all sense and sensation fail to describe the sheer elation in
the lies that it tells.
It as tenacious as oh so many former lovers
and as sweet as the kiss of death.

THE DANCE

O DEATH

The silent speakers
stand like sentries
before the old and broken,
and the records that lie at their sides
rest upon them like weary bodies
awaiting claim.
They guard the relics of a time
proven to have been fleeting
and remain behind like old bones
washed white in the sun,
a vestige of something that used to be alive.
To be dead means one thing and one thing only—
that life once presided.
Life that was,
at some prior time,
weakened,
overpowered,
and snuffed out.
This same condition comes to all of us eventually,
and though we may flout our vitality
and our stamina,
cheat death
and snub our noses at its imminence,
it persists.
It lurks in the shadows of every moment,

SEA GUDINSKI

O DEATH

draws down on every smile,
and hangs like a millstone around our necks
from the instant of our first breath.
Our bodies are merely watches ticking out a life of obdurate length
for which death has lost the key.
We cannot be rewound;
rather, we cycle endlessly
and ultimately slow,
destined for the stillness
from which all animation
has been roused
and to which condition
it is by nature obliged to return.

They say you only live once,
and perhaps this is true.
But while some live many lifetimes in an epoch moment,
some never live at all.
There have been many torrid souls
that have lived their lives
paralyzed by fear,
themselves entirely unaware of the inanity
by which they spend their days.
All those who stand still and wonder,
all those who worry

THE DANCE

O DEATH

and wait with bated breath,
will succumb to death—
most times long before they've comprehended its vastness
or come to terms with its inevitability.
It is the truth that all men must face,
and yet it remains a mystery to us all.
There is no cause to mourn or fear.
Woe to those who die
and yet remain in their bodies;
those whose mortal coil is unaffected
by the emptiness in their breast.
A man whose light has gone from his eyes
and yet continues to see the sun
dies a thousand deaths
before he must shuffle up the steps
to St. Peter.

What must be realized by the least of us
is that all of life is just one long series of blinks—
brief flashes of light
punctuated by lapses into darkness.
We emerge from the void at birth
and slip into it again at the moment of our passing.
There is no preventative measure,
no illusive fountain
that can grant the seeker immorality.

SEA GUDINSKI

O DEATH

Death is the one and only thing that life assures—
the only great comfort we can hold as doubtlessly true.
To be afeared of such a positive is foolish,
is it not?
After all,
at the moment of our birth,
we have already begun to die.

THE DANCE

LOVE AND OTHER HEARTACHES

Hope springs eternal
in the lover's breast.

Vague uncertainties
take on the air of magic.

Impossibilities become
objects of mad desire.

Dreams flourish,
to be dashed at sunrise.

—Oh, but how they dance in the light of the stars,
spurred on by remembrances that cause the heart to flutter
and reason to be blown away with the wind.

She is a picture of restlessness
that causes stolid minds to wonder who and what and why.

A picture of chaos
and peace
that wrestle
intertwined in the night.

A soul unaffected by the grim foreshadowing of eventualities
and the promise of grave disappointments.

One who writes off reason with a glance.

LOVE AND OTHER HEARTACHES

One who searches every moment for the object of her bliss.

One who seems him reflected in the trees
and pavement
and in the faces of strangers.

One who cries at dawn when she wakes to find her soul parted.

One who yearns unconditionally for the attainability of her dreams.

One who begins anew when old memories fade
and prays for their worlds to collide.

She cannot be dissuaded.

She cannot be convinced of the error of her ways
any more than the moon could convince the sun not to rise
in order to grant her one more hour in the sky.

She is forever ebullient,
and her optimism flies in the face of harsh reality.

She finds solace in predestination,
meaning in dissonance
and hope in the charm of the past.

THE DANCE

LOVE AND OTHER HEARTACHES

Her life is like a skyscraper built on the end of a matchstick—

Precarious and unstable,
she spends her days filling its rooms with all her most prized possessions
and carries on throughout the night with perilous haste—

All while knowing full well that if it were to topple,
it'd make waves with the same magnitude
as the Empire State Building falling into the sea.

3AM

White whiskey and wandering hands
To fend off the fear that waits in the dark.
Drinking in stardust and lamenting the plight of man
Two souls wander, lost.

Finger-picking troubadour crossing silent night
Singing forgotten verses, turning back the hands of time.
Once upon a memory there was a light
Gleaming in her eyes.

In the arms of desire, neither stands a fighting chance;
A touch alone substitutes a thousand words.
And an evening's conversation is contained within a glance.
Each asks themselves, is this the moment hence.

Together they search, and with bated breath they kiss;
Eternity sacrificed for an instant of bliss.
I love him, and he loves me;
I never knew how dangerous a laugh could be.

THE DANCE

THE ENIGMA

She stands alone in a courtyard
and whispers softly to herself in a voice that sounds like rain.
Her eyes shine like shimmering mercury.
Her hair flows down her back in swirls
like aged brandy as it splashes into a glass.
Her curves are the envy of Aphrodite.
Her laugh sounds like freedom bells ringing,
her voice is the cry of a caged bird.
She knows not the pull her presence exerts on my soul.
Her warmth invites me closer,
and her intrigue does the same.
She's tied a string around my heart,
and no matter how far I wander,
it always reels me back to her.
Her essence has wound its way into my brain,
and there's no escaping her lures now.

I met her first at a bar built on the corner of Now and Forever.
I asked her for her name and she just shrugged,
yet she pulled from her pocket a ball of yarn
and spun for me the story of her life.
She has toiled and endured,
yet has never known treachery.
She is as jaded as an innocent may ever be,
yet more sagacious than her years could ever allow.

SEA GUDINSKI

THE ENIGMA

She is as upstanding a woman as any that has ever set foot upon the land,
full up of clear kindness and good intentions—
yet she is more dangerous to me than an open flame.
She coaxes out from me words I have not used in years,
stirs in my breast feelings long dormant,
and when she departs,
she leaves me smiling like a schoolboy in spring.

She is as beautiful as the sunrise,
as deep as the sea,
and as strong and fragile as tempered glass.
For me, she sheds her cloak of mystery
and cries out for love,
yet I find when I loosen her outer garments
that she has clothed herself with still more beneath.
She tells me she wants to know my secrets,
but she shies away each time I open my mouth.
Yet, when I lower my defenses,
she rushes in like a summer wind.

She is a temptress most modest,
one who allures with well-strung words
and a fluttering gaze.
She pens verses in a child's hand
and orders her poison neat.

THE DANCE

THE ENIGMA

She beguiles me with her eyes
and captivates me with her badinage.
She is the queen of duplicity,
an existential nightmare,
and yet startlingly simple in her convictions.
She stares off into the void with an expression of searching intent
and wonder
and when she returns to earth,
all she ever does is meet my eyes and smile.

Passion breath escapes her mouth in clouds like cigarette smoke,
her lips are purveyors of untold ecstasies,
and her soul is replete with ancient mystery.
The deeper I get,
the less I understand
and the more I feel.
Reason whirls away in a torrent.
Morals dissolve like delicate morning dew on a hot summer day.
She has stripped me of all my resistance
and laid it bare to rest.
Lifelong notions of right and wrong meld in her presence,
and there is nothing but heaven in her kiss.
For the very first time in my life,
passion has outstripped reason,
and love has conquered fear.

THE ENIGMA

I can hold her for a moment,
but not for a lifetime.
I can kiss her for an evening,
but not for a fortnight.
She is a king size bed with no exit,
and I am a tightrope walker without a net.

THE DANCE

Men are the world's most enigmatic creatures.
They beguile and they enchant,
they offend and they repel.
They are strong,
chesty marvels of nature who strut through the world large and proud—
yet they are timid inside.
Men are the clasp to which women fasten themselves
and thus create love and longing and life.
To be left alone—
they shudder at the thought.
Alienated amongst their peers,
deprived of mental intimacy,
of the emotional confidence of their fellows,
they remain stoic.
Upon their shoulders rests the burden of the world.
They are born into a position of prominence,
of great trust and deliverance,
and yet are not allowed to question their place—
or else sacrifice their honor.
To shrink from responsibility,
they are posited as weak,
to embrace it willingly,
they are regarded as arrogant and ruthlessly ambitious.
From their earliest years,

THE DANCE

fear is rustled into the farthest regions of the mind,
confined and sequestered,
forced to peer through a lonely wicket and reach out only in
periods of despair—
or drunkenness—
as the character allows.

A woman,
to a man,
is reprieve,
solace,
and warmth.
She burns with the vigor which he hopes to embrace
and flames bright with the wisdom which he hopes to absorb.
He does not dare approach her with the passion with which he
experiences these feelings,
or else appear over-eager.
If she be terminally out of reach,
he dies inside,
his flame of passion extinguished by the very smoke it produces
in his heart.
Woman,
to a man,
is a strange mystic—
a being in which hope springs eternal,
in which graciousness and tenderness bloom unconstrained.

THE DANCE

In her he finds peace of mind and a home.
In her he finds joy nonpareil.
In her he finds love.

But what of the man who loves doubly?
He who has one woman who consumes his soul and another who consumes his mind—
both of whom consume his body?
What of the man who knows not what to choose
and of the woman who meets his strife with parity?
Are they sinners inert—to be shunned and estranged from society?
Or are they star-crossed lovers
for whom the lord of karma has reserved a verse for each of them to sing?
Have they been culled from the masses to set an example in the eyes of the world?
Or have they been drawn out to dance?
—To give to one another the love they cannot scrape from any other source?
Wrong or right,
sinful or just,
they traipse and folly,
they grow and believe—
neither commended to more blame or laud than the other.
Together they relish in sanctuary,
and in guilt they writhe alone.

www.ingramcontent.com/pod-product-compliance
Lightning Source LLC
Chambersburg PA
CBHW021952160426
43209CB00001B/8